Karna's Last Battle

Subhadra Sen Gupta

Om Books International

After Bhishma and Dronacharya were killed, Karna became the commander-in-chief of the Kaurava army. He entered the battlefield of Kurukshetra on the seventeenth day on his mighty chariot carrying his giant bow, Vijaya.

As he raised the bow and pulled the string, a loud twang echoed across the battlefield filling the Pandava soldiers with fear.

Lord Krishna driving the chariot of Arjuna, warned his friend, “Among all the warriors of the Kauravas you have to be the most careful of Karna. He is as fine an archer as you and if you are not careful, he could defeat you.”

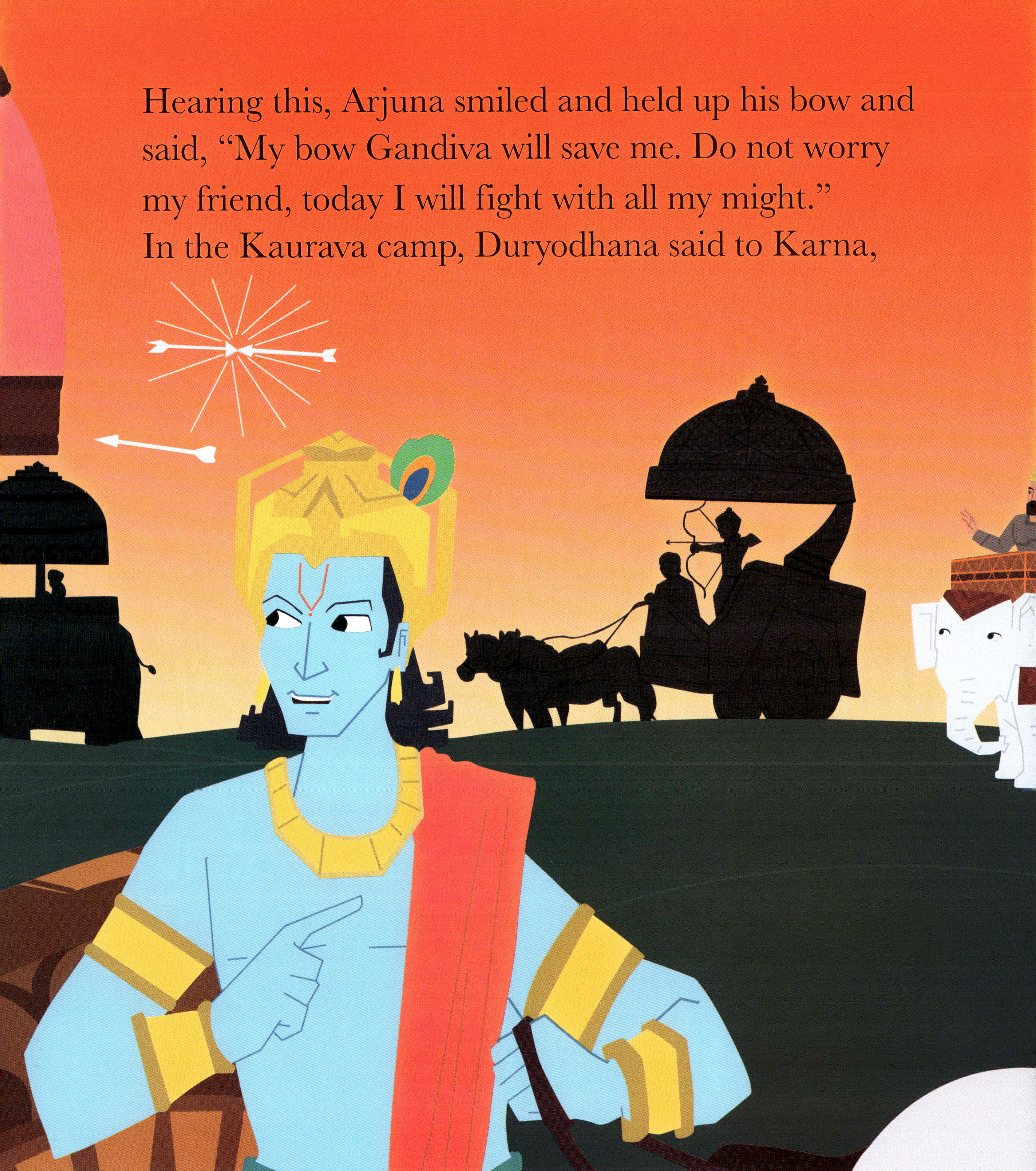

Hearing this, Arjuna smiled and held up his bow and said, “My bow Gandiva will save me. Do not worry my friend, today I will fight with all my might.”

In the Kaurava camp, Duryodhana said to Karna,

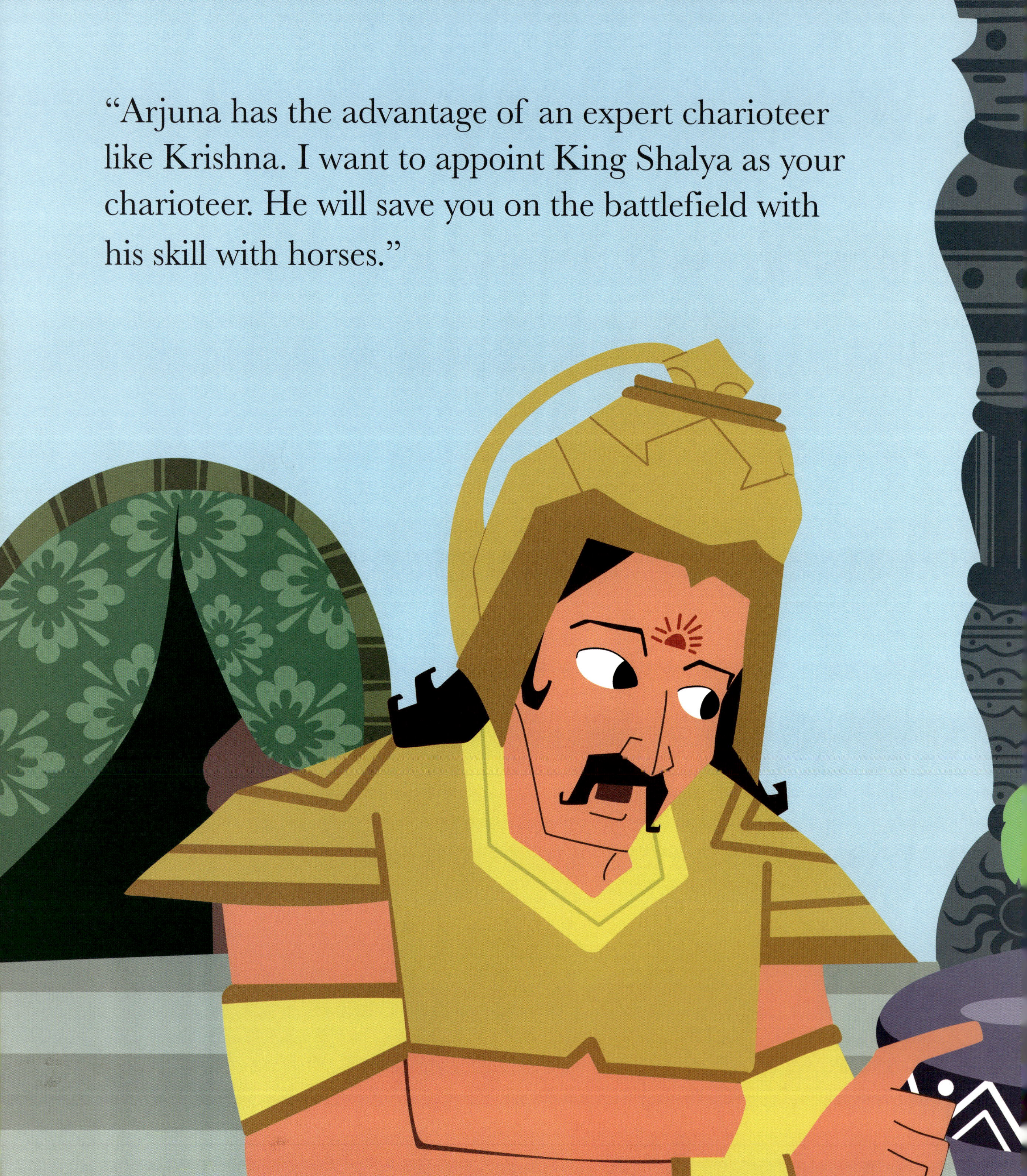

"Arjuna has the advantage of an expert charioteer like Krishna. I want to appoint King Shalya as your charioteer. He will save you on the battlefield with his skill with horses."

Making Shalya the charioteer of Karna was a mistake. Shalya bore a grudge that he, a king, had to drive the chariot of Karna, a charioteer's son. And, he was also annoyed with the fact that Duryodhana had tricked him into joining the Kauravas while he wanted to side with the Pandavas.

At the same time, Krishna had asked Shalya to insult Karna and break his spirit. Riding into the battlefield, Shalya kept insulting Karna and making him lose confidence in his skill as a warrior.

Just before the war, Kunti had revealed to Karna that he was her son and he had promised that he would only kill Arjuna and not any of his other brothers. A mighty battle began between Arjuna and Karna and the sky was filled with arrows.

Karna's dangerous arrow Bhargavastra killed soldiers by the hundreds. He also defeated Yudhishthira, but as promised to Kunti, he did not kill him. Then Karna aimed a dangerous arrow Brahmastra at Arjuna that would surely have killed him.

However, at the last minute Lord Krishna lowered the chariot wheels into the ground and the arrow merely pierced Arjuna's battle crown. So Lord Krishna's quick thinking saved Arjuna and he was ready to fight another day.

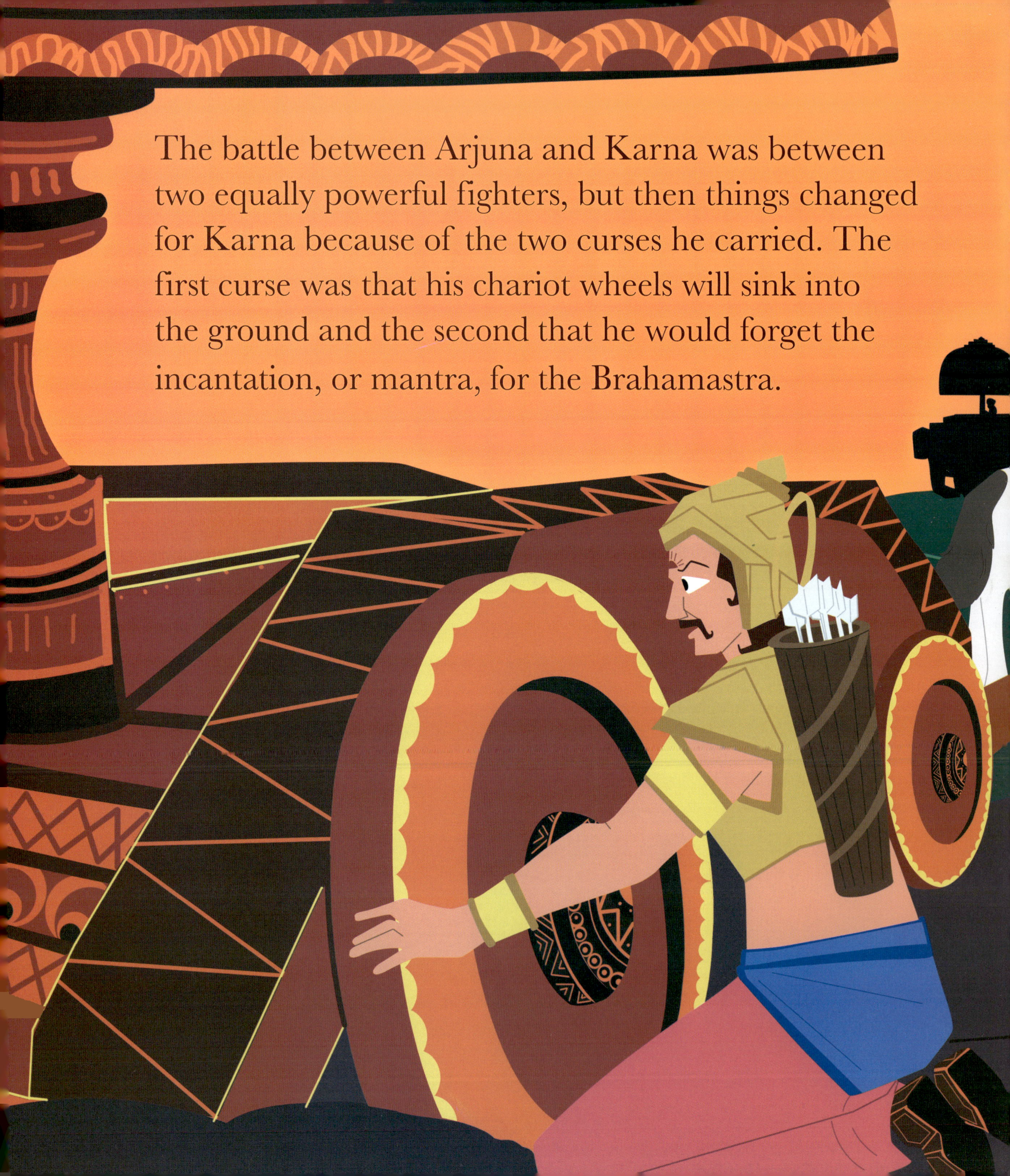

The battle between Arjuna and Karna was between two equally powerful fighters, but then things changed for Karna because of the two curses he carried. The first curse was that his chariot wheels will sink into the ground and the second that he would forget the incantation, or mantra, for the Brahamastra.

As he was fighting, Karna felt the wheels of the chariot beginning to sink into the ground. And, when Shalya refused to help, Karna was forced to get down from the chariot to pull the wheels out.

Meanwhile, Arjuna kept aiming arrows at Karna, he protested, "I am standing on the ground and I am unarmed! It is against the rule of battle to attack an enemy who is not on his chariot." However, Arjuna did not stop. Karna picked up his bow to fight from the ground but at that crucial point in the battle, he forgot the mantra of the Brahmastra weapon. The great Karna died when Arjuna's arrow pierced his chest.

After eighteen days of battle, Duryodhana and all his brothers were dead. So were the five sons of Draupadi. The Battle of Kurukshetra teaches us that greed, violence and war are not the solution to the problems of life. If the Kauravas had chosen to live in harmony with the Pandavas they would not have lost their lives.